ARCHEOPHONICS

ARCHEOPHONICS • PETER GIZZI •

WESLEYAN UNIVERSITY PRESS • MIDDLETOWN, CONNECTICUT

Wesleyan Poetry

Wesleyan University Press
Middletown CT 06459
www.wesleyan.edu/wespress

Frontispiece by Jon Beacham / The Brother In Elysium.
"Untitled Winter #61." Collage, 2015.

This project is supported in part by an award from
the National Endowment for the Arts.

Hardcover ISBN: 978-0-8195-7680-4
Ebook ISBN: 978-0-8195-7681-1

Library of Congress Cataloging-in-Publication Data
available upon request.

5 4 3 2 1

CONTENTS

FOR KENT JONES

Poetry, like music, is not just song.

—JAMES SCHUYLER

ARCHEOPHONICS

Archeophonics

I'm just visiting this voice
I'm just visiting the molecular structures
    that say what I am saying
I am just visiting the world at this moment
    and it's on fire
It's always been on fire

I'm saying this and it's saying me
That's how it works, seesaw like
The archive in the mouth and the archive is on fire
That's the story
The sun and the body and the body in the sun

It was like this just like this
The world that's coming toward me
And the world around me
Around me are words saying this
    saying fire
Saying something or all of it

Field Recordings

For today's tourist, orientation is impossible
—RIMBAUD

LANGUOR

The old language
is the old language,
with its lance and greaves,
broken shields
and hammered vowels;
a stairway ascending
into a mirror—see it
climb the old helix,
beneath a scarred
and chipped northerly sky,
rotunda blue.

Sing genetic cloud forms
mirroring the syntax

in reflection, and what
would you have?

Paving stones, rhetoric,
the coping of bridges,
leanings, what
is taken from *res*?
To reconstruct? To re-
cognize the categories
have failed? That
the index was a lyre.

The lists have grown
lonely, far from home,
houses of worship,
roofs, toy stores and
liquor stores, names,
historical furniture,
descriptions of architecture,
patina in a fanfare city.

I have eaten the air
of that city.

THRALL

The old language
says the apple
is the old apple,
it spoke
in categories
and gave her all
the dance floor
she needed, all
those vocab-
ularies and animal
nights before her,
we see through
to spotted fur.

Lithe, the taut
syllables in apple
and the ecstasy of
naming. Or was it
knowing? Windows
swing open.

The chest
a hammering thing.

This hammering
thing, life as I've
known it, know me,
is over. I might as well
say it. The apples lie
scattered on ground.

The earth reclaims
its booty right be-
fore the eyes. So
swiftly the letters
replace, the
letters dearrange
and uncompose
the self in itself.
The orchestral side
is taking away me.

These letters
no longer anchor.

WRAPPER FRAG

The world today
is slowcore,
a rhythm section
dragging.

At the moment
I drag and solo
in a bitten landscape,
torn vowels
that sound out vowel
or sadness like glitter
sprinkled in a mind.

A sun-slashed parking lot,
thinking a poem
stalled
in the broken
surround.

See the chubby kid dazed,
his spilled bike,
more debris,
CVS in the distance.

Remember me
to convenience stores.
I saw this too
every life of my day
yet I ate, I had money,
and a car.

WIND INSTRUMENT

There were markets
used bookstores
trellises and brick.

These were the words
I could see
thinking of the body.

It's strange here
all the names in me.
The gain and its foliage.

In my last rotation
it was hard to tune in.
The dial was faulty.

The static lovely.
It spoke to me
through a grubby transom.

Was that a cathedral bell
or the air conditioner?
Crisp air coming in.

Looking out the frame
I studied grass.
So many pages blank.

It's hard to look that close.
I watched from a high window
while I slept.

GLITTER

Faces fly by
in random litter,
as September rays
hit the lawns.
The high-lit
dry white shafts
slightly vintaging.
The bright
horizon preening
in fife air.

The days go and
are gone.
The night's gone
before us,
a neon cursive glow.
If only to dream
awhile, through

an ascending scale
of history, its ill be-
gotten schemes,
statecraft, unwieldy
theatrical devices.

The old language
renews the pundits'
chatter, can sometimes
bunch in groups,
power jumbotrons,
or one's laughter
in particular.
Just now, out
the car window
paper flags
and ballots kite.

Feel the parade
air on your skin.
A cotton shirt
touching it. The
manufactured rays
are ancient, fall

through a time-gone
ticker tape array.
The floats and whorls
and banners above.

The old language
dozing in sun.

STRANGENESS BECOMES YOU

The old language is
the old language.
It don't mean shit.

It's not where you begin
it's how you finish.
Everyone's got beer muscles
when they're young.

Try as you must.
Break as you will.
Solo in space
clinging to space.

Fuck, the air said
passing a corner,
a long ropy snot
hitting a gutter.

To know something
and fail.
Why discount it?
The onslaught of eyes
beneath a fuck-you sky.

The syntax breaks down
its mangled draft and says,
one day the poor
will have nothing
to eat but the rich.

I hate that, when syntax
connects me to the rich.

REVERB

I hate how syntax
connects me to shit,
or say the day
is jeweled and burning,
the fires banking,
and none of its letters
produce the horror
at the heart of the index.
The old document
hangs over the twinned
stair of murder
and something else—
that original slap of glove.

The project is archival,
all that blood in the mouth.
The old language
could have told you,
it's too late,
we watched you die,

watched you move
through shocking losses
and the solo flight
you are taking back
into the old language.

It's the same but different,
different now.
The mouth knows the bit,
the taste of it.

A NOTE

It's strange here, all this time in me and time around me. I was trying to climb out from under 5AM thinking outside the truck and its engine are real.

Today the slinky is 70 years old. Next year my body will be 57: it was human, it was American, it was a piece of big data, it was employed, it loved and mourned the documents behind a people.

In my time I loved people.

RIME

It was a language to eat the sky
a language to say goodbye

standing with others
standing in the dust.

The old language
continues its dialogues

in ordinary dust.

When Orbital Proximity Feels Creepy

Right now there are teenage microwaves
screaming through your body
while you are having text with me.
This is the moment I'll need you to sing
     with me.
I am making my way in some dark room
looking for other structures to love.
From the left something speaking
     I can't identify.
The floor goes unfixed and moving
and this doesn't happen only at night
but during the day when I don't want
     to think on it.
That I saw a blood-orange ball caught
     out my window.
That I'm listening to light and it said time.
I'm listening to time, it says, ha.
You need to be howling at bloody torn space.
Need to be spooked out of your hidey-hole
     and its glowing mess.

But I love this ball I'm riding on.
The strange hunk of metal and rock whizzing
    around my loves and my loving.
The fact I spin and it spins and everything
    is spinning close up.
From far away it's so cool.
I guess they call this physics or they call it laws.
If they're so well-made, why do we suffer?
I thought the day was opening
but now I see it's already gone.
Outside the cruel dove has a broken window.
The day isn't friendly.
Who are you to me?
A way to understand the floor?
The floor that holds me up and leaves me
    standing.
I don't know where to go.
Me, Tuesday at 5PM.
What does it mean to be in a room,
    any room.
The wind banging against the clapboard.
I know enough to see the cracked pane
isn't going to be fixed anytime soon.

Who has time for such things in the song?
Breaking. Blooming.
The wobble of light on wood-grain late
    in the day.
In the loneliness of orange.
In the loveliness of orange.

Release the Darkness
to New Lichen

But I found a way to say no
to the wood in my house

it kept creaking
wouldn't stop talking

I found a way to say no

I need to be standing
in the warmth of the wood
that the sun made

I need to find myself dissolving

otherwise it is all otherwise
I'm lost, did I say that

I saw the frill of light today
walking on the path

could you hear the stirring
in the wood, pine needles
and the branches

was it wind or a creature
am I here or is it over

this was the first day
the nothing day
in the nothing year

it gave me courage

it gave hints of blue,
clouds, electrical
and dancing

it gave me rays
I've never seen

shooting down
touching things

this was the first day

A Social History of Mercury

In oneself the ghost of self

The walls where I live

Floorboards in spotted light

To see oneself clearly

The mirror world

Its cruel repetition

This is not a melancholy state

Simply primeval

Words live here

Take root

Their vocative flourish

"the winter sun says fight"

The winter sun says fight.
The arctic blasts say fight.

This polar world is flat
even if my head
says round. Like this
meant something
to me, like nothing.

I was more ing
these days to
every surface. So
what's in this morning
that will solace?

Once I saw the city
of God reflected
in a freak shadow
the sun cast. I
thought life complete,
tight, happiness.

Now sun says cigarette,
and I abide. I remember
its noisy ray clanging
my room on my knees
looking for crumbs.

I remember days and
nights and days and
nights, days, nights,
high and dirty.

Now fog says coffee,
that'll bring you back.
To where? Where
do I actually live so far
outside my head deep
inside the chemical
wash of my genes.

I am fighting for love
but I need a new god.

Left here, this one
no longer fits. I, sick
of the reptile in me,
the dis in time,
its twigged agony.

I've been here before.

This World Is Not Conclusion

When I look out your window I see another window
I see a wedding in my brain, a stylus and a groove
a voice waving there

When I look out your window I see another window
these trees are not real they grow out of air
they fell like dust they fell

So singing is seeing and vision is music
I saw diadems and crowns, daisies and bees, ribbons, robins,
    and disks of snow
sprung effects in pencil-light

When I look out your window I see another window
I see a fire and a girl, crimson hair and hazel eyes
a public in the sky

When the world comes back it will be recorded sound
that cooing shrub will be known as dickinson
the syllabic, fricative, percussive, and phatic will tear open

Out your window I see another window
I see a funeral in the air I see alabaster space
I read circumference there

Night Work

The eyes take their relief in dark
in this night room seeing things.

The waking dark old-like
a monk's pagoda in some far bell country never seen.

To have never seen it in me ringing
the night room the gone steps creaking ens.

To remain like this
what the world wants.

The motor fumbles in the distance
anything becomes rhythm in the distant wave.

You can ride it if you can hear it
the whine of night the ongoing ribbon.

Song

I want color to braid,
to bleed, want song
to fly to flex to think
in lines. To work
the pulp, to open up
this cardinal feeling
in green.

The hardest part
is the songbirds
and their fugue state,
fug state, fuck it.
The world is neon
in the gloaming quiet.

I am willing to walk
away, willing to be
on fire, to blaze
to Blake, to sink
into the moon's

aphorism and
its garden of figures.

The moon above
my life. It's rough
and real tonight,
cold fusion
reflecting sun.
There is a quaver,
a gibbous light
to this equation.

Puzzling rays full
of dinghies, pixies,
kobolds, and gems,
heroes, songsters,
and your face.
The strangeness
becomes you,
darling night.

Google Earth

Taking in the earth from wide space; to see its incommensurate blue; I am also thinking of your face, its dark wilds always, its burning incandescent blur; it wasn't the sky exactly, it's more like the sky an arrow takes; I once texted all I really see is your face; the world is broken down tonight, when you're far I don't like the sea, don't like these clouds either, the tree's canopy, don't like these touch screens majestic with distance.

Rainy Days and Mondays

Over the all this and
under the all that

between this yes
and that yes

hauntedness

between the girl
and arrows

the long ago
and far away

between galaxy
and litter

talking to myself
for now

a song

Instagrammar

These lost stars
tomorrow
will they be
there when we
wake in our
sorrow, is it us
so lost in the
moment,
is it today
we look
to flower

If it were
because the time
we saw and
loved, if it was
because we are
and should be
this, the way
it was then, we
find it glowing

this our future
and bravado

We say how
could this be
when did this
happen that
we'll find ourselves
somewhere else
in some future
laughing, why
is it incompatible
I mean what does
it matter, whether
the ship were in
the trees or
the ground was
in the water

The stars doubled
in the river
the stars once
floating in past
futures we ran

to, if it all
seems dizzy
and mayhem
if it all seems
promised and
ordained

Our future is
in the air

Antico Adagio

Bring down the lights. Bring out the stars. Let the record sing; the vibraphone; the violin; the gong. We call this charm a festooned gazebo in twilight. We call night and her creatures to the summer screen; every beat a wheel every wheel aglow. The soft tight musical light a freshet. And happy who can hear the wood, the ferns bobbing, the stars splashing down. I wanted this glad tight happy light inside the gloaming. I wanted glow. The piping anthem of a voyage listing in lamplight, oboe light; hear it and fly. Hear it fly like friendship like modernism beginning like a steamer pulling out to sea in an old reel dreaming. Married to a song; to a pebble of song.

Pretty Sweety

Here there are small animals
foraging and content

Perhaps this is what's called
perhaps love is a small animal foraging

content entirely with its mouth there
with the ant and the sun and fur

This is a strange view
sunlight and furlight and a mouth

busy with nature
a mouth busy with its bloom

a mouth blooming loveliness

A Ghosting Floral

To be dispatched
by downcast eyes

To have forgot
a singularity in green

It's not what you think
when I look

The vista suits me

Loam fanning out
into music falling

Shadows wheel

Wings drafting above
doing it finding it

The day suits me

The air inside me
inside you, things

Do not move
let the wind speed

A Garden in the Air

You wonder summer's terabyte,
here on the terra forming,
floating and atomizing,
giving over to shadow,
then a muffler rumbling,
distant engine, a little cozy,
acoustic shadowing,
or when the bells
die out slowly, like light
across the neighborhood's
plumbago skies,
a blanket feeling
in the face of narrative,
a map on somebody's face
suddenly changing
from the time it takes
to the time it takes,
and you keep thinking,
overhead the ancestral
chirring, this twilight's

creaturely bluing feels
downright numerical,
like polka dots
on the ceiling, still
you're thinking how
this chirring and
its attendant evening,
erratic nothings, a material
weaving, warping, excess
jetting, ancestral airs,
what you are speaking,
leaves, whirring, living,
listing, in summer green,
how can the tonic sustain
its frequency, moment
of tuning, but
you do all the talking,
you do all the talking
and forget the world,
in this room, the walls,
what you are speaking,
these fires at the edge.

Sentences in a Synapse Field

For I wanted sound / to
dig into sound

For snow and blood / for
wine and mirrors / for
electrons / and electricity

For debris / for damaged art / our
collective fortune / future

For as long as there have been soldiers / there
have been poets / for as long as poets
there has been a bridge

For I wanted to hold a room in silence
For debris flooding back into a wave

For as long as particles / a charge / for
it should be incredulity / to be alive

For these things that can be told / until
mystery becomes elegy

For it was March going into April / for
the day was / speaking the day

For what you thought / for
what you buried / for
who you are /

How to Read

FOR ROSMARIE WALDROP

A world of light and a world of openism

A syntax of heat and dynamism

A human world mewling in the dark

A giganto space of silence, time

A mind on fire in the heat of the quest

Rhythm percussion assonance

Energetic silent magic

A textual nimbus, air born

Civil Twilight

Life is big these days and it's hard to take
    its measure.
It's a complicated phrase
this planet we're on.
But what if it were all water
    on stones, plash.
Pine bows creaking like ropes
    on a clipper ship
in some shitty weather of yore.
This ball in space emitting cries
    into space.

If I saw you and the I said,
    my poetry is changing,
I would say my life is changing.
I see it there clearly as power lines
    above a rail-yard playing wind.
The notes are where I take shape
and then arrive into the present
    world-station, hello.

It didn't matter that the whorl
didn't happen as it did.
That the speckled horizon
couldn't be otherwise.
This is what I'm saying now,
so I'm going deeper and it burns,
    a better whisky,
the sky turning monarch into night.

But earlier the light was witchy,
instamatic and shining, 6 degrees over
    the horizon every day.
The sun in this world on its way
from my porch in the west.
There is song in the grass
against the whine of the jet.
It all evaporates and decays,
not into silence but into life.

What if it were all music?
What if the day were a countertenor
informing us, besting bureaucracy,

offering sustenance against my case of the punks.

Take the ride, it won't take you all the way.

The sun in the street or am I just lucky.

The day was like that.

And the established fact of the sun.

A Winding Sheet for Summer

1.

I wanted out of the past so I ate the air,
   it took me further into air.
It cut me, an iridescent chord
   of geometric light.
I breathed deep, it lit me up, it was good.
All these years, lightning, rain, the sky,
   its little daisies.
Memento mori and lux.

2.

And you can't blame me.
This daisy-feeling.
I was a poet with a death-style of my own
    waking.
I occupy the rest of it.
A blue-green leaving feeling.
To no longer belong to a body sometimes
    open to air.
In rain, in early morning rain.

3.

Today was the day of the amphitheater in mind.
The day of a dreaming speech where the light is dope
    and that's all you can say.
When a feeling degrades and evolves into thought like
    2AM dilated, revealed a star.
It will say this long agony is great being awake.
It is being lovely now.

4.

All the stars are here that belonged to whatever
    was speaking.
I built my life out of what was left of me.
Sky and its procedures.
A romanticism of clouds, trees, pale crenellations,
    and poetry.
A musical joybang.
Touching everything.

5.

When the words come back their fictions remain.
Thunderheads and rain, lexical waters raking gutters,
    carving a world.
The stylus will live in the flash.
A daring light from pewter to whatever.
Now discrete observations produce undramatic sound,
    like I am a bubble,
make me the sea. O, make me the sea.

6.

For a long time the names of things and things unnamed.
For a long time hawks and their chicks, fox and their cubs,
   mice and their mice.
For a long time bunnies and boojum, and a name
   for every bird in me.
I am native to feathers—their netherside.

7.

The sun was a goldish wave taped to a book.
A wavy diagram in a fusty book.
Foxed old wave.
A soft electro-fuzz enters the head.
A soft fuzzy opiate lightness.
What could be the message in this
    pointillist masquerade.
What use memory.

8.

I came from a different world.
I will die in it.
Someone saw it, I love them for seeing it.
I love seeing it with them.
Love watching it die in me.
It wasn't behind or beside me.
Finding it wasn't it.
Being it was everything.
That was the thing I thought as I fell.

9.

I am that thing in morning, whatever motors in the skull,
   something is claimed.
Sudden rain keeps it real.
Rooftops from the window look stunned.
   Cleansed.
Looking out over the day, the pale performing day.
I always consult the air before composing air.

10.

And what have you been given, the blue nothing asks,
    who are you under clanging brass?
Who are you, Saturday; sing to me.
See the crows thread summerismus.
Afternoon shade mirrors an issuelessness.
A perfection of beetle slowly treading summer's blade.
The leaves broadcast color.
I was born in summer, my conqueror,
    breaking into wisteria.

II.

The sun was a golden rag nailed to a ladder.
And here the marigolds grow down to the banks.
The mayflies drowse above water.
How then the dazzling surface and its dictions
    under piled clouds,
and clouds sitting there by place and sound.
One thing. This thing and sound glitters.
Indicative transitive particular battles the void.
All afternoon a green-gold silent light
    on the spotted grass, sprung.

12.

I know it's summer even if I can't decipher the call.
I believe in the birds haunting me. I held on.
I'm full of bluster but also full of vision.
I'm not ready to put the book down.
To stop singing bright spots thrilling the quicksilver
    over my torrent.
I make sounds, forget to die. I call it living,
    this inhuman conch in the ear.
A pewter sensation and wind.

13.

The sun remains a yellow sail tacked to the sky.
I am climbing air here. I am here
   in the open.
The kestrel swerves.
Its silent kerning.
A stunning calibration of nothing.
I'm left to see.

Bewitched

When I look
to the east
I could not
find you
in the west
where the light
was dying you
were not there
northerly the sky
grew pitch
silence to the south
there was
only billowing

Now to go over
to greet
the small wind
as the huge
blows by
horn blind
and feathered

what is this
former swaying
this deep pomp
beyond and
waiting
crouched and
magnified

Is the word
a cunning bird
even in new
dark I will not
be quiet, the
feathering
covering me
I will not turn
away showing
my face and
love the words
pouring from
your mouth

Po-lyph-o-ny it was
a music to me
a freaky effluvium
entering me lit
with that speak
with its thick
embryonic music
born into a strange
new light darker
than any like
I had known
before, polyphony
spoke to me

It was a
language
to eat the sky
a language
to say goodbye
standing
with others
standing in
the dust

the old language
continues its
dialogues in
ordinary dust

Now the sun was
a bower of
rusty cables
its deep center
flashing, welding
this room
to silence
an ascension
hard and hauling
heaves above
the time and
its tether

When I think
all you have
done I
think on all
of this and you

know the way
I trod the path
dissembled
with leaves
under the ghosting
shades an elm made
and discovered
the pages of
my book
open to greet me

In the poem
I am thick
with dream
my limbs heavy
forcing myself
to wake into
striated dusks
rising through
the stratum
a question
in my brain

ACKNOWELDGMENTS

My thanks to the editors where these poems first appeared:
*A Public Space, The Baffler, BOMB, Cambridge Literary Review,
Granta, Harper's, Jubilat, The Los Angeles Review of Books, The
Nation, The New Yorker, New York Review of Books, Paris Review,
Poetry,* and *Yule Log.*

Poems have also appeared in limited-edition chapbooks, my
thanks to the editors: Rod Mengham for *Field Recordings*, Cam-
bridge UK: Equipage Editions; C.W. Swets for *A Winding Sheet
for Summer*, Amsterdam NL: Tungsten Press; and Anthony
Caleshu for *The Winter Sun Says Fight*, Plymouth UK: Periplum
Editions.

"How to Read" appeared in the festschrift *For Rosmarie
On Her Eightieth*, editors Ben Lerner and Anna Moschovakis.
Brooklyn: Ugly Duckling Presse.

"This World Is Not Conclusion" appeared in *A Mighty
Room*, edited by Michael Medeiros, Amherst: Emily Dickinson
Museum.

"Song" appeared in *Best American Experimental Writing*,
editors Charles Bernstein and Tracie Morris. Middletown:
Wesleyan.

Thanks to the folks at MacDowell Colony and Cambridge University for time and focus.

Many thanks to Rae Armantrout, Dan Bevacqua, Hannah Brooks-Motl, Alan Gilbert, Kevin Killian, Ben Lerner, Joseph Massey, Drew Milne, Amanda Petrusich, Pam Rehm, Jon Ruseski, and Geoffrey Young; my biggest thanks go to Kent Jones, Suzanna Tamminen, and Lydia Wilson, for their crucial part.

ABOUT THE AUTHOR

PETER GIZZI is the author of six collections of poetry, most recently, *In Defense of Nothing: Selected Poems 1987–2011*, and *Threshold Songs*. He has also published several limited-edition chapbooks, folios, and artist books.

His honors include the Lavan Younger Poet Award from the Academy of American Poets, and fellowships in poetry from The Fund for Poetry, The Rex Foundation, The Howard Foundation, The Foundation for Contemporary Arts, The John Simon Guggenheim Memorial Foundation, and the Judith E. Wilson Visiting Fellowship in Poetry at Cambridge University.

He works at the University of Massachusetts, Amherst.